UNDERSTANDING

METAPHORS

Crabtree Publishing Company

www.crabtreebooks.com

BY
R. JOHNSON

Crabtree Publishing Company
www.crabtreebooks.com

Author: Robin Johnson

**Publishing plan research
and development:** Reagan Miller

Photo research: Margaret Amy Salter

Editorial director: Kathy Middleton

Editor: Anastasia Suen

Proofreader and indexer: Wendy Scavuzzo

Cover design and logo: Margaret Amy Salter

**Layout, production coordinator and prepress
technician:** Margaret Amy Salter

Print coordinator: Margaret Amy Salter

Photographs:
All images by Shutterstock

Metaphors featured on cover:

Middle left: to zip your lips (keep quiet)

Middle right: a cash cow (a product or business that
someone makes money regularly from)

Bottom left: to have your head in the clouds (to be unaware
of what is going on around you)

Bottom right: a wolf in sheep's clothing (someone with bad
intentions pretending to be good)

Library and Archives Canada Cataloguing in Publication

Johnson, Robin (Robin R.), author
      Understanding metaphors / Robin Johnson.

(Figuratively speaking)
Includes index.
Issued in print and electronic formats.
ISBN 978-0-7787-1776-8 (bound).--
ISBN 978-0-7787-1876-5 (paperback).--
ISBN 978-1-4271-1617-8 (pdf).--ISBN 978-1-4271-1613-0 (html)

      1. Metaphor--Juvenile literature. 2. Figures of speech--
Juvenile
literature. I. Title.

PN228.M4J64 2015   j808'.032   C2015-903959-2
                                         C2015-903960-6

Library of Congress Cataloging-in-Publication Data

Johnson, Robin (Robin R.) author.
  Understanding metaphors / Robin Johnson.
      pages cm. -- (Figuratively Speaking)
  Includes index.
  ISBN 978-0-7787-1776-8 (reinforced library binding) --
  ISBN 978-0-7787-1876-5 (pbk.) --
  ISBN 978-1-4271-1617-8 (electronic pdf) --
  ISBN 978-1-4271-1613-0 (electronic html)
  1. Metaphor--Juvenile literature. 2. Figures of speech--Juvenile
literature. I. Title.

  PE1445.M4J64 2016
  808'.032--dc23
                        2015026810

Crabtree Publishing Company
www.crabtreebooks.com   1-800-387-7650

Printed in Canada/112015/EF20150911

Published in Canada
Crabtree Publishing
616 Welland Ave.
St. Catharines, ON
L2M 5V6

Published in the United States
Crabtree Publishing
PMB 59051
350 Fifth Avenue, 59th Floor
New York, New York 10118

Published in the United Kingdom
Crabtree Publishing
Maritime House
Basin Road North, Hove
BN41 1WR

Published in Australia
Crabtree Publishing
3 Charles Street
Coburg North
VIC, 3058

CONTENTS

WHAT IS A METAPHOR?

Have you ever been called a chicken? You don't have feathers or make clucking sounds, do you? But maybe you get scared sometimes. A chicken gets scared sometimes, too. It is afraid it will be made into stew! You and a chicken can both get scared, so you have something in common.

If someone calls you a chicken, he or she is using a **metaphor**. A metaphor is a **figure of speech** that compares two unlike things. It describes something by showing how it is the same as something else. The two things are different in most ways, but they share an important **characteristic**.

A characteristic is a feature or quality that identifies a person or thing.

FIGURATIVE OR LITERAL?

We use two types of language when we speak and write. We use **literal language** to describe things as they really are. We say, "Our teacher is strict. He gives us extra homework if we misbehave." These sentences state facts which are true. The teacher really is strict. He really does give extra homework for bad behavior.

We also use **figurative language**. This type of language takes words beyond their normal, literal meanings. We say, "Our teacher is a tyrant! He gives us a mountain of extra homework if we misbehave!" The teacher is not acutally a tyrant. A tyrant is a harsh or cruel ruler. But tyrants and teachers both make people follow rules. And the teacher does assign extra homework for bad behavior, but it isn't actually piled as high as a mountain.

We use both literal and figurative language to tell our stories.

LITERAL

"I've got more homework now than I've ever had before!"

The first sentence is literal and does not compare unlike things. The second sentence is figurative. It uses a sea metaphor to describe the amount of homework. Do you *sea* the difference?

FIGURATIVE

"I'm drowning in a sea of homework!"

IS IT REALLY A METAPHOR?

We use metaphors to paint pictures with words. Metaphors let writers describe things in creative ways. They help readers imagine **characters** and **settings**. Characters are the people in a story. The setting is where a story takes place.

We also use other types of figurative language to tell our stories. **Similes** are almost the same as metaphors. Like metaphors, similes are figures of speech that compare two unlike things. But, unlike metaphors, similes use the words "as" or "like" to make their comparisons.

Look at the sentences below. Some have metaphors. Some have similes. Others have no figures of speech at all. Compare the sentences. Notice how they bring the characters to life in different ways.

Zoe's braids were two skinny black snakes slithering away from her head.

Zoe had thin black braids in her hair.

Zoe's braids were as wild and wiggly as little black snakes.

The first sentence has a metaphor because it says something is something else. The second sentence does not have a figure of speech. The third sentence has a simile because it uses the word "as" to compare unlike things.

William always had a smile on his fac[e]

William's happy smile was like sunshine on a cloudy day.

William's smile was a streak of red paint on his face.

The first sentence is literal becau[se] it does not have a figure of speech. The second sentence has a simile because it uses the word "like" to compare unlike things. The third sentence has a metaphor because it compares unlike things without usi[ng] the words "like" or "as."

ABOUT THIS BOOK

This book is divided into sections to make learning about metaphors a breeze.

FIGURE IT OUT! Studies metaphors in different types of writing.

TALK ABOUT IT! Uses discussion questions and graphic organizers to get you thinking and talking about metaphors.

WRITE ABOUT IT! Includes samples and tips to help you create original work.

NOW IT'S YOUR TURN! Gets you to make your own marvelous metaphors in poems and stories.

FIVE STEPS TO WRITING

1. **PRE-WRITING:** **Brainstorm** new ideas. Get creative and shower your paper with words.

2. **DRAFTING:** Your first draft might be a disaster. You can clean it up later.

3. **REVISING:** Cover your bases and take advice from other writers. It will make your work a big hit!

4. **EDITING:** Be a walking dictionary and check your work for spelling mistakes.

5. **PUBLISHING:** Share your sweet work with family and friends. It's a piece of cake!

METAPHORS IN POEMS

Have you ever met a metaphor? You will often find them in poems. Most poems are short. They tell a story in just a few lines. Metaphors let poets paint pictures with few words. They also help poets set the **mood** of their poems.

Read the passage below. It is the beginning of a poem about a thief on horseback, called a highwayman, who robbed travelers on the road in olden times. Notice how the poem makes you feel—even if you don't understand all the words!

The Highwayman
The wind was a torrent of darkness among the gusty trees,
The moon was a ghostly galleon tossed upon cloudy seas,
The road was a ribbon of moonlight over the purple moor,
And the highwayman came riding—
    Riding—riding—
The highwayman came riding, up to the old inn-door.

—Excerpt from "The Highwayman" by Alfred Noyes

TALK SENSE
Many metaphors rely on the five senses. They make comparisons based on how things look, smell, sound, taste, or feel. How might readers rely on their five senses to make sense of "The Highwayman"?

8

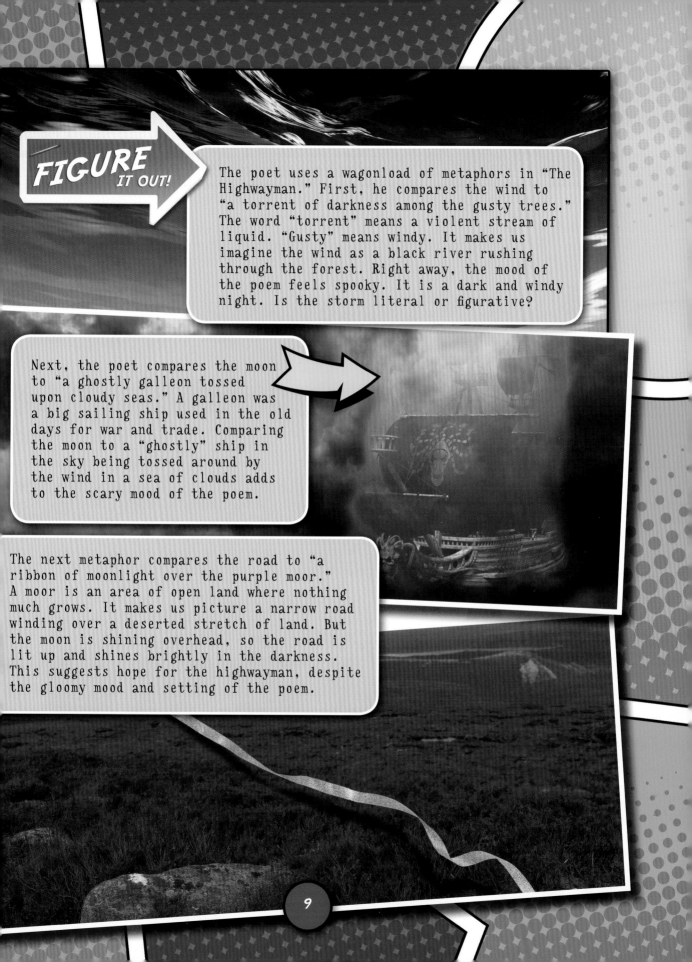

FIGURE IT OUT!

The poet uses a wagonload of metaphors in "The Highwayman." First, he compares the wind to "a torrent of darkness among the gusty trees." The word "torrent" means a violent stream of liquid. "Gusty" means windy. It makes us imagine the wind as a black river rushing through the forest. Right away, the mood of the poem feels spooky. It is a dark and windy night. Is the storm literal or figurative?

Next, the poet compares the moon to "a ghostly galleon tossed upon cloudy seas." A galleon was a big sailing ship used in the old days for war and trade. Comparing the moon to a "ghostly" ship in the sky being tossed around by the wind in a sea of clouds adds to the scary mood of the poem.

The next metaphor compares the road to "a ribbon of moonlight over the purple moor." A moor is an area of open land where nothing much grows. It makes us picture a narrow road winding over a deserted stretch of land. But the moon is shining overhead, so the road is lit up and shines brightly in the darkness. This suggests hope for the highwayman, despite the gloomy mood and setting of the poem.

Andrew wanted to practice writing metaphors. He wondered what would happen if he changed the comparisons in "The Highwayman." Would that change the mood of the poem? He used his five senses to come up with some new lines.

First, Andrew thought of a metaphor to describe the moon. He wanted to paint a peaceful picture, so he thought of lights that make him feel calm at night. Sometimes he sleeps with a nightlight when he feels scared, so he chose that as his first metaphor.

Then he thought of ways to describe the wind. What if it blew gently? How would it feel on his face? What else touches his face gently? When his mother kisses him goodnight, her lips feel soft on his forehead. Andrew decided to use that as his second metaphor.

Finally, Andrew thought about the road. Is it always spooky to travel at night? Coming home from grandma's house isn't scary. The sights and sounds of the road are familiar to him. So is his favorite book at bedtime. He decided to use that metaphor to tell his story.

THE FIVE SENSES

sight	touch	taste	sound	smell
Moon is...	Wind is...		Road is...	
a nightlight	a mother's kiss		a favorite bedtime story	

WRITE ABOUT IT!

Andrew joined the words in his senses chart to make some metaphors. Notice how they change the mood of the poem. How do you feel when you read the first three lines of Andrew's poem?

The wind was a mother's kiss on a child's forehead,
The moon was a shiny nightlight, glowing by a bed,
The road was a favorite story, waiting to be told...

NOW IT'S YOUR TURN!

Brainstorm your own metaphors for the wind, moon, and road. Does the sound of the wind remind you of a wolf? Is the moon the shape of a soccer ball? Does the winding road give you the same feeling you get on a roller coaster? Use your five senses to come up with some creative comparisons. Then put them all together and take the reader for a ride!

METAPHORS IN SONGS

You hear metaphors all around you. They may even be in your favorite songs! Some songs say "you are my sunshine" or "you're a firework." Others tell you that "love is a battlefield" or "life is a highway." Listen carefully and you will hear musical metaphors everywhere!

Like poems, songs are short. Singers use a limited number of words to express their feelings and tell their stories. Read the short song below. You've probably sung it many times before! But did you know it has a metaphor in it? See if you can spot it.

Row, Row, Row Your Boat
Row, row, row your boat,
Gently down the stream.
Merrily, merrily, merrily, merrily,
Life is but a dream.

The writer of this song compares life to a dream. We have dreams while we are sleeping, so the metaphor helps paint a sleepy, lazy picture. How would the song have sounded without the metaphor? Not so dreamy!

Row, row, row your boat,
Slowly on the lake
Merrily, merrily, merrily, merrily,
Life's a piece of cake.

We can also imagine the song with different metaphors. The writer could have said, "Life is a sunbeam." That would have painted a warm, sunny picture. Or maybe, "Life is just ice cream." That would have made the song a bit sweeter. There are so many words you can choose when you write. The choices you make show the reader your **voice**.

Voice is the unique personality of each writer.

TALK ABOUT IT!

Sydney wanted to make some metaphor music, too! She used "Row, Row, Row Your Boat" as a model. She brainstormed some ideas for her song. She could write about her pet. "Walk, walk, walk your dog." She could write about her favorite sport. "Catch, catch, catch the ball." Sydney uses a wheelchair, so she decided to put that in her song.

Then Sydney thought of metaphors for life. She wanted to show that life is fun and moves quickly. She thought of other things with the same characteristics. Roller coasters are fast and fun, and so are sports cars. She wrote her ideas in a word wheel.

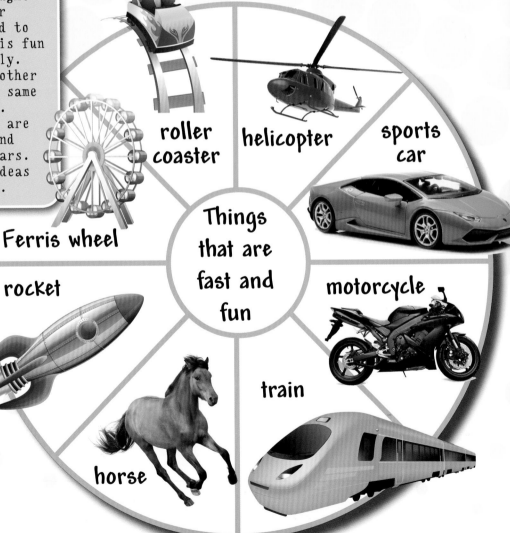

roller coaster

helicopter

sports car

Ferris wheel

Things that are fast and fun

motorcycle

rocket

train

horse

Sydney chose a Ferris wheel for her metaphor. She wanted to show that there are ups and downs in life. You may get scared along the way, but the ride is always fun! (She was going to use a roller coaster for her metaphor, but the only word she could rhyme with it was "toaster"!)

Roll, roll, roll your chair,
Turn and laugh and squeal.
Round and round and round you go,
Life's a Ferris wheel.

NOW IT'S YOUR TURN!

Use "Row, Row, Row Your Boat" as a model to write your own short song. Brainstorm ideas to replace rowing a boat. Then think of metaphors for life. You could say that life is a dance or a bowl of candy or anything else! Show your voice in your writing. Then use your voice to sing your song!

METAPHORS IN NOVELS

You have seen that metaphors make songs and poetry more imaginative. But they are also perfect for **prose**. Prose is spoken or written words told in sentences. Prose is used in **novels**, short stories, and plays. Writers often use metaphors in prose. The passage below is from the novel *Little Women*. The characters are dreaming about the future. Here is Jo's **dialogue**.

"Wouldn't it be fun if all the castles in the air which we make could come true, and we could live in them?" said Jo... "I'd have a stable full of Arabian steeds, rooms piled high with books, and I'd write out of a magic inkstand, so that my works should be as famous as Laurie's music. I want to do something splendid before I go into my castle, something heroic or wonderful that won't be forgotten after I'm dead. I don't know what, but I'm on the watch for it, and mean to astonish you all some day. I think I shall write books, and get rich and famous, that would suit me, so that is my favorite dream... I've got the key to my castle in the air, but whether I can unlock the door remains to be seen," observed Jo mysteriously.

—Excerpt from *Little Women* by Louisa May Alcott

Metaphors bring stories to life. This boy must be reading *The Jungle Book*!

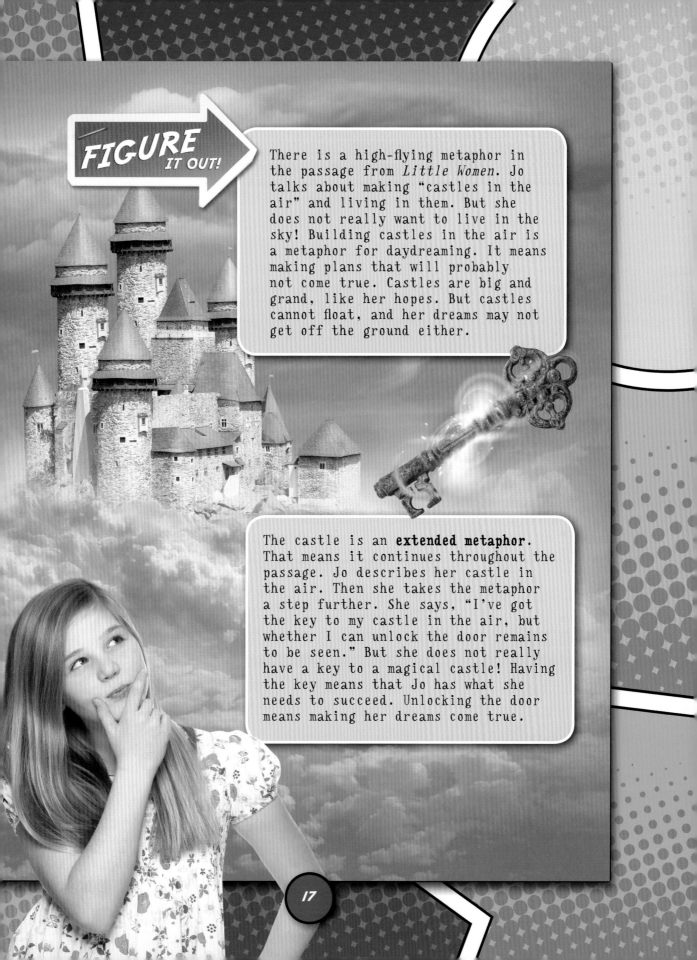

There is a high-flying metaphor in the passage from *Little Women*. Jo talks about making "castles in the air" and living in them. But she does not really want to live in the sky! Building castles in the air is a metaphor for daydreaming. It means making plans that will probably not come true. Castles are big and grand, like her hopes. But castles cannot float, and her dreams may not get off the ground either.

The castle is an **extended metaphor.** That means it continues throughout the passage. Jo describes her castle in the air. Then she takes the metaphor a step further. She says, "I've got the key to my castle in the air, but whether I can unlock the door remains to be seen." But she does not really have a key to a magical castle! Having the key means that Jo has what she needs to succeed. Unlocking the door means making her dreams come true.

Jo's castle in the air reminded Tyler of another metaphor. Have you heard people say your home is your castle? Your home is not really a castle—unless you are a prince or princess! The metaphor means your home is special. Tyler wanted to take the castle metaphor a step further. He wrote an extended metaphor comparing his home to a castle.

Tyler brainstormed all the ways his home is like a castle. His dad is the king, his mom is the queen, and his baby brother is the court jester! A jester is a person who does silly things to amuse the king and queen. Tyler jotted down his ideas in a castle chart.

Metaphors let you paint pictures with words!

HOW MY HOME IS LIKE A CASTLE

Tyler = prince

Dad = King

Mom = queen

baby brother = court jester

flower garden = moat

big dogs = dragons

neighborhood bullies = enemy Knights

crib = dungeon

throne = couch

Tyler used his castle chart to write a gem of a story. Do you think it is fit for a king?

My home is my castle. Mom and Dad are the king and queen. They rule over me and my baby brother, our silly little court jester. As the prince, I protect our lands from dragons who want to bury bones in our yard. I also helped the king dig a moat around the house to keep enemy knights out—and to plant the queen's flowers in. The court jester makes us laugh, but if he throws his toys, he gets put in his dungeon for a time-out. But the queen always lets him out to watch TV beside her on the throne.

NOW IT'S YOUR TURN!

Now it's your turn to bring it home! Think of a metaphor to describe your house. Is it a train station, with people coming and going all day long? Is it a library, a quiet place with lots of books? Is it a jungle, full of wild animals? Keep the comparison going throughout your story to make an extended metaphor.

METAPHORS IN HISTORICAL DOCUMENTS

Metaphors have helped people share their true stories throughout history. We find metaphors in old journals, letters, and other important **nonfiction** documents. Some of the most powerful metaphors are found in documents about the Underground Railroad.

In the 1800s, thousands of African-American slaves traveled on the Underground Railroad. It wasn't a real railroad, though. And people didn't really travel underground! The word "underground" means hidden. "Railroad" was a metaphor for a network of secret routes and hiding places throughout the United States. Slaves used the Underground Railroad to escape to freedom. This letter is about the journey of some of those slaves.

MR. STILL:—*My Dear Sir*—I suppose you are somewhat uneasy because the goods did not come safe to hand on Monday evening, as you expected—consigned from Harrisburg to you. The train only was from Harrisburg to Reading, and as it happened, the goods had to stay all night with us, and as some excitement exists here about goods of the kind, we thought it expedient and wise to detain them until we could hear from you. There are two small boxes and two large ones; we have them all secure; what had better be done? Let us know. Also, as we can learn, there are three more boxes still in Harrisburg. Answer your communication at Harrisburg. Also, fail not to answer this by the return of mail, as things are rather critical, and you will oblige us.
G.S. NELSON.
—From *The Underground Railroad* by William Still

William Still

FIGURE IT OUT!

Can you tell that the letter is about runaway slaves? No! It sounds as though someone is sending packages by train. Metaphors in the letter hid its real meaning. Using metaphors helped the slaves and abolitionists communicate without being caught. Abolitionists were people who wanted slavery to end. Some abolitionists helped slaves escape to free states and Canada.

So what did the letter really mean? The writer says that "the goods did not come safe to hand." The word "goods" normally means food, clothing, and other things you buy. In the Underground Railroad, it was a metaphor for escaped slaves. They were also called "packages," "cargo," and "boxes." In this shipment, there were "two small boxes and two large ones." Small boxes meant children and large boxes meant adult slaves.

The writer mentions a train from Harrisburg to Reading. Most escaped slaves did not travel by train. They would have been spotted by slave catchers. Instead, the slaves traveled in wagons or on foot. The train stations were metaphors for hiding places along the way. Slaves rested in safe houses, barns, churches, and in other "stations" and "depots."

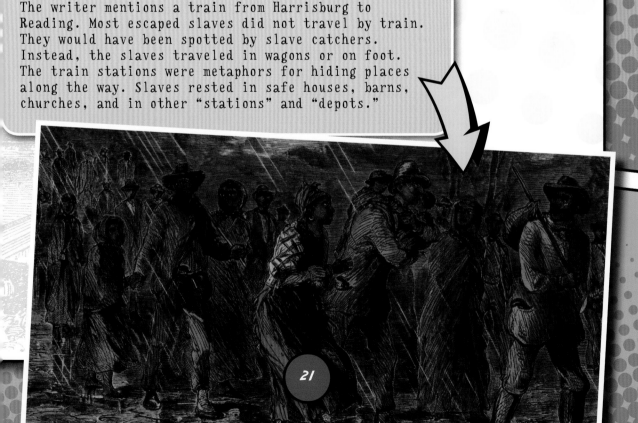

TALK ABOUT IT!

Olivia wanted to write a letter with metaphors, too. She thought about her own travels. She had taken the bus to her grandfather's house. She had flown to an amusement park in Florida. She decided to write about a road trip she took with her family. She used a flowchart to plan her work.

TOPIC: Road trip!

Mom made us pack our suitcases.

We crammed into our little car.

We balanced luggage on our laps.

Dad drove for hours on the highway.

We jumped out of the car the second we arrived.

Olivia wanted to use an extended metaphor to make her story colorful. And what is more colorful than a circus? She thought of all the ways her road trip reminded her of a circus. They were all squished into a small circus car. The family were jugglers tossing the luggage back and forth. And there was lots of clowning around!

Olivia put all her colorful ideas together to write a letter. Read it and enjoy the show!

Dear James,

Our road trip was a circus! Mom was the ringmaster, in charge of the whole show. She had us jumping through hoops to get ready. Then she crammed us into our little clown car. We juggled our luggage on our laps the whole way. Dad was a tightrope walker, following the thin line down the highway. When we finally arrived, we were acrobats bursting from a cannon!

Love,
Olivia

Now it's your turn to write a letter. Think of a trip you took. Use a flowchart to plan your work. Then add metaphors to make it interesting. Was the freeway a parking lot? Was the airport a zoo? Get creative with your travel tale. Someday it might be an important historical document!

METAPHORS IN SPEECHES

Without metaphors, writers would be speechless! They could not write or deliver their best **speeches**. A speech is a formal talk given to an **audience**. An audience is all the people who hear or read what you wrote. Metaphors make speeches sparkle. They also help speakers win over their audience.

This is part of a speech by U.S. President Barack Obama. He gave the speech when he first became president. Notice the metaphors in the passage. They are positively presidential!

America... let us brave once more the icy currents, and endure what storms may come. Let it be said by our children's children that when we were tested we refused to let this journey end, that we did not turn back nor did we falter; and with eyes fixed on the horizon... we carried forth that great gift of freedom and delivered it safely to future generations.
—U.S. President Barack Obama, Inaugural Address, January 20, 2009

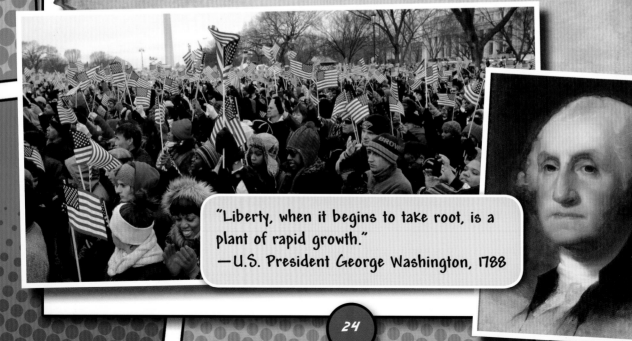

"Liberty, when it begins to take root, is a plant of rapid growth."
—U.S. President George Washington, 1788

24

FIGURE IT OUT!

The first part of President Obama's speech uses a weather metaphor. He asks America to "brave once more the icy currents, and endure what storms may come." The weather was not really bad in Washington that day! President Obama is comparing the country's challenges to stormy weather. Storms and problems can both be scary. But there are always sunny skies ahead.

The next part of the speech uses a travel metaphor. The President says, "we refused to let this journey end," and "we did not turn back nor did we falter." The word "falter" means to hesitate or be unsteady. President Obama is comparing the country's progress to a journey. There are ups and downs and twists and turns on any road. But America keeps on going.

The passage ends with a third metaphor. The President says, "we carried forth that great gift of freedom and delivered it safely to future generations." He compares freedom to a gift. Imagine you are going to a birthday party. You pick out a special present. You wrap it in beautiful paper. You carry it carefully so you don't drop it. That is how freedom looks to President Obama.

TALK ABOUT IT!

Grace wrote a speech, too. She was running for class president. She wanted to convince the other students to vote for her. Grace started by making a list of her characteristics. She is flexible. She is strong. Then she thought of other things with the same qualities. Gymnasts are flexible. Tow trucks are strong. She wrote down those words in another list.

MY CHARACTERISTICS	THINGS WITH THE SAME QUALITIES
(hardworking)	bee, beaver, workhorse
fun	party, beach, park
(determined)	climber
(flexible)	gymnast, rubber band
sweet	candy, ice cream
(strong)	ox, diamond, tow truck
stubborn	mule, toddler
funny	comic book, clown
honest	judge, Girl Scout
(pleasant)	flower, sunshine

Grace read over her list of characteristics. Which ones would make her a good leader? She circled those qualities. She would include them in her speech. The second list would help her write some metaphors.

Grace used her lists to write a short speech. She included lots of metaphors so it wouldn't be boring. Would you vote for her?

I would like to tell you why I would make a good class president. I am a rubber band. You can pull me in different directions and I won't break. I'm as strong as a diamond. I am a climber. I keep pushing through tough problems and reach for the top. I am a workhorse. I will work hard for the class. I am a flower. I take a seed of an idea and grow it into something beautiful. I hope you will choose me!

NOW IT'S YOUR TURN!

Now it's your turn to earn some votes! Pretend you are running for class president. Make a list of your best qualities. Think of other things with the same characteristics. Then use the lists to write a winning speech.

In the next chapter, you will see how other students helped Grace improve the metaphors in her speech!

REVISE YOUR METAPHORS

You are a metaphor machine! You brainstormed ideas and wrote first drafts. Now you can move on to the next steps—revising and editing your work. Use this handy guide to help you master your metaphors.

METAPHOR REVISION CHECKLIST

1. Do your metaphors compare two unlike things?

2. Do your metaphors make comparisons without using the words "as" or "like"?

3. Do your metaphors rely on the five senses?

4. Do your metaphors help paint a picture for the reade

WORK TOGETHER

You think your metaphors are magic. But maybe you can make them even better! A good way to revise your work is to let other students read it. They will tell you if your metaphors are mixed up o marvelous. Do they paint a pictur or muddle up your story? The group can help edit your work, too. They might spot spelling, grammar, and punctuation mistakes you missed.

MAKE IT BETTER

Grace read her speech to a small group of students. She wanted their input before she shared it with the whole class. The students liked her speech but had some suggestions to make it even better.

Tyler pointed out that the diamond sentence used the word "as" to make a comparison. That made it a simile, not a metaphor. He also mentioned that diamonds are both strong and sparkly. Olivia suggested that Grace use a bee metaphor instead of a workhorse. Then she would not repeat the word "work." Andrew thought it would be clever to use the word "pick" instead of "choose," since the last metaphor was a flower.

Like a good president would, Grace listened carefully to their suggestions. She agreed that they would improve her speech. So she made the changes to make her work better.

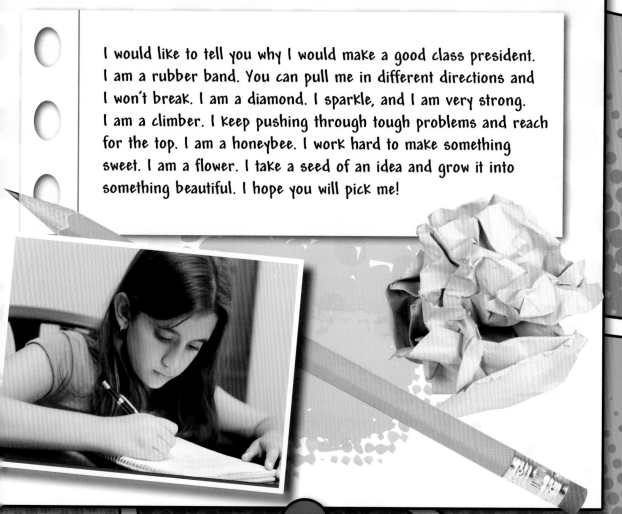

I would like to tell you why I would make a good class president. I am a rubber band. You can pull me in different directions and I won't break. I am a diamond. I sparkle, and I am very strong. I am a climber. I keep pushing through tough problems and reach for the top. I am a honeybee. I work hard to make something sweet. I am a flower. I take a seed of an idea and grow it into something beautiful. I hope you will pick me!

PUBLISH YOUR METAPHORS

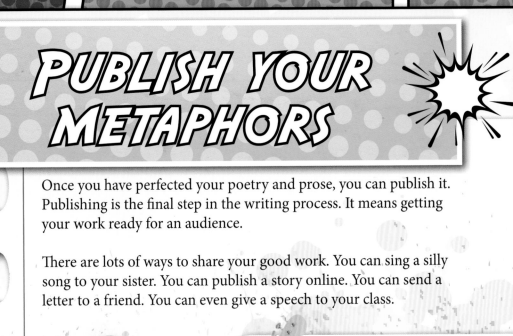

Once you have perfected your poetry and prose, you can publish it. Publishing is the final step in the writing process. It means getting your work ready for an audience.

There are lots of ways to share your good work. You can sing a silly song to your sister. You can publish a story online. You can send a letter to a friend. You can even give a speech to your class.

You may think that public speaking is a nightmare. You stomach might be in knots. But don't be frozen with fear! The audience will be glued to their seats. Your words will be music to their ears. You're a rock star!

LEARNING MORE

BOOKS

Similes and Metaphors by Ann Heinrichs. Child's World, 2010.

Snowboarding Similes and Metaphors by Gail Herman. Gareth Stevens Publishing, 2009.

You're Toast and Other Metaphors We Adore by Nancy Loewen. Picture Window Books, 2011.

WEBSITES

Fling the Teacher Simile and Metaphor
https://kmott.wikispaces.com/Fling+the+Teacher+Simile+and+Metaphor
Build a teacher and then answer metaphor questions to fling him away!

Kids Educational Games
http://www.turtlediary.com/grade-4-games/ela-games/shoot-for-metaphors-and-similes.html
Play a game to test your knowledge of metaphors and similes.

IXL Identify Similes and Metaphors
www.ixl.com/ela/grade-4/identify-similes-and-metaphors
Test what you have learned by taking this similes and metaphors quiz.

The Underground Railroad
http://teacher.scholastic.com/activities/bhistory/underground_railroad/
Learn more about this important metaphor and the people who used it.

GLOSSARY

Note: Some boldfaced words are defined where they appear in the book.

audience The people who read or hear your work

brainstorm To think of many ideas, often in a group

character A person in a novel, short story, or play

dialogue The words spoken by characters in a story

extended metaphor A comparison that continues throughout a poem or story

figurative language Words with meanings that are different than their basic, literal meanings

figures of speech Words or phrases that are not used in the usual or literal way

literal language Words that state facts or describe things as they really are

metaphor A figure of speech that describes something by calling it something else

mood The tone of a story or poem that makes the reader feel a certain way

nonfiction Prose writing based on facts, real people, and real events

novel A long book of fiction with characters and action

voice A writer's personality that shows in their word choices

INDEX